Sixteen Things To Do Before The Judgment

8. 12. 5. 3. 10. 2. 1. 6. 15. 14. 11. 9. 3. 7. 4. 16.

MCWHORTER

Published by Christian Day Publishing Company

6148 Jones Road, Flowery Branch, GA 30542

ISBN 13: 978-1-7336624-8-2

Published in the United States of America

2020 – First Edition

Glad You Could Make It...

If we knew when we would die, odds are we would make every attempt to get ready to meet God.

Most will not get ready. In fact, most probably do not know what getting ready entails.

If you don't, don't make the mistake of not finding out.

This book exists to help you bring your faith in sync with the clear tenets of the Bible.

It is not advisable to presume you know what God expects of you, regardless of whether your presumption is based upon the teachings of a well respected and loved person or has been gained from your own researched opinions.

The Holy Bible can be trusted above the

opinions of men.

With these things in mind, it is my prayer and sincere hope that you will take these sixteen points to God in earnest prayer for confirmation or denial. Only His Spirit can give you confidence that you are hearing truth, whether in this book or any other.

What is the scriptural reality of being a Christian? What does that really look like? And what does God expect of those who follow Jesus Christ?

Most of the expectations God has for Christians are impossible for human effort. But, fortunately, God provides all we need in Christian life to meet His expectations, **if we desire them enough to ask for His help in meeting them**.

It is not easy for the natural person to follow Jesus Christ, because we must walk away from our own lives in order to live His life.

How can a prospective believer justify leaving his own life behind? It must be weighed in the balance against the huge benefits and wisdom of following Jesus.

Have You Evaluated Your Present Life in the Light of Eternity?

Here is a brief list of criteria for evaluation:

- Is eternal life with God worth more than your temporary life on earth?

- Are the superficial treasures of this world in any way comparable to the eternal treasures in Heaven?

- Given the fact that all humans are born in sin, and ineligible, on their own merits, for eternal life, are you willing to risk standing before God with nothing but your sinful nature to show for righteousness? Or do you want to have Jesus vouch for you before God as a true follower of Himself?

- Is eternal life worth giving up your own will to do God's will for a few decades – or however much remains – of this life?

These are the kinds of decisions we face when we evaluate a life of following

Jesus, versus continuing to live according to our own desires and preferences.

The following sixteen undertakings are the landscape of a genuine and mature Christian life. Each seems impossible from the perspective of the natural mindset. Therefore, it's necessary to acquire the perspective of Jesus Christ. That happens when you love truth enough to make the Bible your daily bread and primer for wisdom, and the Holy Spirit your Teacher and Guide.

Most of the "To Do's" on this list are mandates from God. Look in each chapter for the scriptural injunctions that identify them as vital, as you pursue the character of Jesus Christ in your daily walk toward a life very pleasing to God.

And remember, for those expectations of God that seem to be impossible, you will need to ask for His grace to enable you to fulfill His desires for you.

These sixteen topics are not concepts to

merely think about and understand; they're to be acquired, made part of your life.

Now, you might encounter resistance from any traditional thoughts you might have acquired and from the addictions of the old life to leisure, being in control, personal pride, or vanity. If you suspect these old lifestyle patterns will have to go in order to "make room," so to speak, for these new life acquisitions, you are absolutely right.

What, precisely, has to go? Everything that opposes these sixteen scriptural characteristics and injunctions.

But don't worry. When you weigh the old lifestyle patterns in the balance against the value of what you will gain here, the former things are – as the apostle Paul said – *DUNG*. More politely, the things that oppose these steps toward God are unprofitable to life in Christ.

Isn't eternal life with God worth it?

It is!

That is to say, *He* is!

So, I urge you to not hold back, nor to look back.

Go after God's will with all your heart.

CONTENTS

1. Repent and Believe Jesus Christ

Jesus preached repentance.

But what is that?

The root meaning of repentance is to "re-think." But the emphasis in scripture is on radical rethinking – a 180-degree reversal of thinking. And not just a one-time re-thinking that ruminates over Jesus' offer of salvation and eventually returns to former ways of thinking. Scriptural repentance is permanent re-thinking, the kind that signals a clean break from old ways of thinking.

This re-thinking is the genesis of acquiring the thought life and mindset of Jesus Christ. Here's what God told the prophet Isaiah for us:

"For my thoughts are not your thoughts, neither are your ways my ways, saith the LORD. For as the heavens are higher than the earth, so are my ways higher than your ways, and my thoughts than your thoughts." Isaiah 55:8

God describes the huge gulf between His way of thinking and our human way of thinking. He wants us to cross that gulf, to come over to His side. That is why we are told to *"Let this mind be in you, which was also in Christ Jesus."*

Your thought life is fundamental to everything that follows; your thoughts shape your beliefs; your beliefs shape your words; your words shape your actions; your actions produce your lifestyle.

For your lifestyle to change into something like that of Jesus' lifestyle, you must give up the old in favor of this new way of thinking.

That is repentance.

Repentance is often considered an emotion. Believe me, it can be a very emotional thing to realize that your life is so far away from the love, truth, faith, and goodness of God that you need a radical overhaul, and that even your way of thinking has been wrong. Repentance reveals to us the depths to which our thoughts have taken us in dishonoring God, our loving Father and Creator.

To think that He gave His very own Son to die for you and me! What a heartbreaking, and yet, heart-mending thing for God to do!

He did it for you.

Hebrews chapter six tells us that "repentance from dead works" is part of the foundation of our life in Christ. Foundations are what we build things on. What will be built upon the foundation of repentance?

As mentioned before, your beliefs, your words, actions, and lifestyle will be built on it. So, repentance must be deep and solid; it has to support a great edifice: a "house" built upon the Rock.

The Gospel message of Christ's sacrifice for you is highlighted all through the Bible. It is alluded to and foreshadowed in the Old Testament and brought to reality and fruition in the New. Start reading the New Testament, and preferably, in the book of John.

Allow the Holy Spirit to move upon your heart as you read. Don't read it as though it's required for a school exam; read it as though it is required for a life exam. Which, it is.

"Jesus came into Galilee, preaching the gospel of the kingdom of God, and saying, 'The time is fulfilled, and the kingdom of God is at hand: repent ye, and believe the gospel.'" Mark 1:14-15

The time has come. As we near the return of Jesus Christ, it is more and more apparent that He is coming soon. He asked this question regarding His return, *"When the Son of man cometh, shall He find faith on the earth?"*

Each of us has to consider how we will respond to His question.

Will we begin to walk with Him in faith? Once started, will we *continue* to walk in faith? And ultimately, when we have walked with Him over time and under circumstances, will we continue walking with Him when we feel a heavier weight of those circumstances?

Repentance extends far beyond the first emotional realization of how wrong we have been. It remains strong in our hearts, sustaining us each time we have our original decision confirmed by the reward of God's presence in our lives, and as we taste the goodness of His grace and mercy toward us.

Repentance is radically turning over your mind to the mind of Christ for retraining and reforming in the fire of His loving truth and under the skillful workmanship of His Spirit.

If you have never repented of sin, I urge you to ask God for the grace to do it now.

If you have repented, begin to live a life of repentance, continually adapting your thoughts to the mind of Christ, and asking your Father's forgiveness whenever you miss that goal.

You can do all things through Christ who strengthens you.

2. Be Born Again, a New Creation

"Except a man be born again, he cannot see the kingdom of God... Ye must be born again." John 3:3, 7

Many have wondered, as a man named Nicodemus did, What is this thing Jesus spoke of, this being born again?

From the scripture above, we see it is a mandate, a non-negotiable condition of entering the Kingdom of God.

Given the nature of the mandate, it is odd that we find people who have professed Christianity for years of their lives, yet who have never been told that they "must be born again" or that being born again is a condition of entry into eternal life.

Many who have heard the term, have

said, "Oh, that's some Protestant terminology," or "It's what Baptists call 'believing.'"

Don't let that mandate from Christ Himself be watered down in your mind. Being born again is the starting point of the new life that is in Christ Jesus.

He explained it further this way: *"That which is born of the flesh is flesh; and that which is born of the Spirit is spirit."* (v. 6)

Jesus meant this: You were born into this natural world a natural person; to enter the spiritual world of Heaven, you must be born into it, and that only happens by the Holy Spirit of God coming into your heart to give you a new heart and new life.

That is a miraculous occurrence; it does not come simply by changing your mind – repenting. While repenting is turning over your thought process to God for renewing, being born again is turning over your entire life for regeneration, making it new.

Repentance of your sins against God gives you an open door to Jesus. He died to pay for your sins, so repentance gives you the opportunity for His forgiveness, the wiping away of all charges against you. His forgiveness makes you clean so that the Holy Spirit has a "clean vessel" to occupy. When you give your life over to God, having been cleansed of your sins, the Holy Spirit will enter your heart and begin the work of transformation that Jesus spoke of.

The reason for your forgiveness is to make possible the process of changing you, which the Holy Spirit undertakes in your life. If you were not cleansed of sin, the Holy Spirit could not come into your heart and make it new.

Some people have thought that salvation is simply "getting a ticket" to heaven, engendering no change whatsoever in one's life. But that would negate the plan that God revealed by His prophets. For example:

"A new heart also will I give you, and a new spirit will I put within you: and I will take away the stony heart out of

your flesh, and I will give you an heart of flesh." Ezekiel 36:26 (spoken more than 600 years before Christ)

"*And I will give them one heart, and one way, that they may fear me for ever, for the good of them, and of their children after them:*" Jeremiah 32:39 (spoken about 650 years before Christ)

The new life God designed for followers of Christ to live is actually the life of Christ. His life! That is what Paul expressed when he said:

"*I am crucified with Christ: nevertheless I live; yet not I, but Christ liveth in me: and the life which I now live in the flesh I live by the faith of the Son of God, who loved me, and gave himself for me.*" Galatians 2:20

You might rightly ask, Does that mean, then, that I have to die to have this new life?

Yes, but we are given this benefit: God considers that the crucifixion of Christ accomplished our crucifixion. With our commitment to Jesus, we are saying to

God, I voluntarily place my old life on the cross with Christ, so that I no longer desire its sinful nature, its sinful way of thinking and acting, or the terrible, eternal fate that sin had procured for me. I willingly walk away from who I was, my goals, my dreams, my own will, and I gladly submit my life to You and Your will, for whatever purposes you might want to use me.

That is the meaning of the scripture that says, *"What? know ye not that your body is the temple of the Holy Ghost which is in you, which ye have of God, and ye are not your own? For ye are bought with a price: therefore glorify God in your body, and in your spirit, which are God's."* 1 Corinthians 6:19-20

Being born again is often compared to an ideal marriage between a man and a woman. Ideally, love induces one person to marry another. That same love induces that person to become one with the beloved one, meaning that each spouse dies to self in order to become one with the other. Ideal marriage is intended to be a union for life, as salvation is intended to bring union between man and God.

If you have been happily married, you understand the concept of dying to self for the sake of love.

When you view being born again from God's perspective, of desiring union with Him, its absolute necessity is clear. You MUST be born again.

(For further insight into this union, read the seventeenth chapter of John, and give your life fully to God through Christ.)

3. Humble Yourself

"Every one that is proud in heart is an abomination to the LORD." Proverbs 16:5

You and I both know that you are not God. You are His created being. Made from soil. Every good thing you have previously thought of as your own – your intellect, skills, talents, abilities, possessions that, perhaps, you bought and paid for, and more – are among the blessings you have received from God. You have merely been a steward of those benefits.

It may seem stark and cruel to break that to you in this way, but in case you were not aware, many people consider themselves to be their own god, capable of handling whatever comes their way.

God does not approve of that sort of dishonest thinking because it makes mockery of His role in your existence.

Not that you considered yourself your own *actual* god, but the fact is, every human relishes the role of being the master of his fate and the captain of his soul. Boss over his or her lifestyle, decisions, and choices. That fact is part and parcel of why we tend to resist the truth of God until we gain a degree of understanding and trust.

Especially in America is this true, where everyone has been exposed to the "I can do it," "nobody tells me what to do," "I pulled myself up by my bootstraps," self-made-man, entrepreneurial/competition syndrome.

That being said, in many places, it is a cultural irregularity to have no pride in accomplishment.

But in the Kingdom of God, He detests pride. If anyone deserves to be proud, it is He. Yet, He is not proud. He is holy.

Once you know that "God resists the proud, but gives grace unto the humble," that knowledge can bring a measure of wisdom, enabling you to recognize what produces a successful tenure under His Lordship.

In short, God hates the pride of mankind. Not only that, He desires you to have such understanding that you, too, will hate it.

Proverbs 16:18 tells us, *"Pride goes before destruction, and a haughty spirit before a fall."* It is good to be forewarned about pride, and it is even better to know the advantages, in God's Kingdom, of humility, though it is not highly prized in the world, and, in fact, not even in some churches.

Contrary to popular belief, humble people are not weak people, especially those who humble themselves under the mighty hand of God. They recognize that He is the Source of their strength and wisdom.

For example, Paul said that when he asked the Lord to remove his thorn in the flesh, the Lord told Him, *"My grace is sufficient for you, for my power is made perfect in weakness."* To that, Paul remarked, "*Most gladly therefore I will rather glory in my weaknesses, that the power of Christ may rest on me.*" 2 Corinthians 12:9

The Bible tells us that Moses was the meekest man on earth (Numbers 12:3), yet he is renowned as one of the world's greatest figures.

It is not difficult to humble yourself before such a great and mighty God as ours. Only pride can hinder us from doing so.

I urge you to get rid of pride and humble yourself. Doing that will give you a huge advantage in your life of following Jesus Christ.

Not doing it?

Well, that will lead to destruction.

4. Be Filled with the Holy Spirit

When a man or woman has been delivered from sin, self-love, addictions, anger and so many other faults of the human condition, it is not good to remain empty. God's desire is to fill a new believer with the Holy Spirit.

Not every pastor or teacher wants their congregants to be FILLED with the Spirit, for they have prejudices against the things that can happen in a person's life when full of the Spirit. For example, when believers in the book of Acts were filled with the Spirit of God, they began speaking in tongues, casting out devils, preaching boldly in the streets, laying hands on the sick, and, generally going way beyond the norm, and, as for today, way beyond the characteristics of many of our staid, sleepy American churches.

Perhaps these leaders are afraid wildfire

will break out and they won't be able to
rein it in.

In actuality, we must not be ruled by
tradition, but by the very Holy Spirit
many are afraid will get out of their
control.

God had sound reasons for desiring that
the followers of Jesus be filled to
overflowing with the Holy Spirit. For
example, the worldwide Church actually
needs the power of the Spirit that is
manifested through His gifts and fruit
when He is honored in our midst.

The Holy Spirit is the One who offers
gifts cited in 1 Corinthians 12 – gifts
such as words of wisdom and
knowledge; gifts of faith, healing, and
working of miracles; prophecy,
discerning of spirits, various kinds of
tongues, and the interpretation of
tongues.

All of these gifts are needed in the
Church; otherwise, God would not have
made them available. His Word says the
gifts of God are "without repentance,"

which means they are irrevocable. In other words, He has not taken them away.

Those who prefer only a "mild dose" of the Holy Ghost say that when you get saved, you get all of the Holy Spirit that you need. What they mean is, stay calm, be obedient to your leaders, find yourself a comfortable place to hide in the congregation, pay your tithes, and don't rock the boat. And, for Pete's sake, don't start saying God *told* you something; do you want people to think we're all crazy?

Okay, that is not what this section is about. God does want you to be filled with the Holy Spirit. He wants you to trust the Holy Spirit completely, love Him, listen to Him as well as talk with Him, learn from Him, follow Him.

He is to be the Guide for your life, your Comforter, Teacher, your everything!

So, as soon as possible after you are born again, ask Jesus to fill you with the Holy Spirit of God. You need His power!

Do not settle for a mild touch from Him.

Desire the fire and fullness of His presence.

Traditional thinking will suggest that, because Jesus was filled with the Holy Spirit, we don't need to be.

But Ephesians 5:18 advises us, *"And be not drunk with wine, wherein is excess; but be filled with the Spirit."*

Be FILLED with the Holy Spirit, and let Him have His way in your life!

5. Love God with *ALL* YOUR BEING

God does not allow competition for His Lordship.

Certainly, before we were born again, you and I were highly accustomed to obeying only one individual: Self.

Your self was your boss and your loving enabler because he or she would permit you to do whatever you wanted.

But remember, as a born-again person, you are no longer your old self; you have a new self. Paul wrote this: *"If any man be in Christ, he is a new creature: old things are passed away; behold, all things are become new."*

You are a new creature. That was the deal. In order to live forever, you had to give up the old self, who was on the way to hell anyway, because of sin.

So, now you have a new Boss. He died to save you from your sin. If you truly believe that, you will love Him far more than you love your old self.

In fact, that is what God expects to be true of you. Read this:

"*Thou shalt love the Lord thy God with all thy heart, and with all thy soul, and with all thy mind, and with all thy strength: this is the first commandment.*" All.

Next, read this word from Jesus:

"*If any man come to me, and hate not his father, and mother, and wife, and children, and brethren, and sisters, yea, and his own life also, he cannot be my disciple.*"

The word, "hate," here, means to love far less. Note that all those Jesus said you must love far less than Himself are those who have had strong influence over your life, but that now must never be allowed to compete with Him for your attention and deference. And that group includes your OWN LIFE!

Ask yourself this question: Does God deserve to be my Lord and Master, to tell me what I can and cannot do?

Well, that's a good question. Let's see, He created you out of clay. We've established that He *is* God; you're not. He made the universe and probably knows a whole lot more than you. He has the power and authority to decide who measures up to His standards and who does not. And He died so that you can live forever.

So, yes, He qualifies.

Because the kind of all-out, reckless, all-consuming love for God described in scripture is the first and greatest commandment, we have to conclude that it is "ground zero" for Christianity. That means **if you and I have not subjugated everything in our lives to the doing of that primary thing, we are not yet obeying Him**.

We encounter all sorts of demands in our lives and all sorts of opportunities, including opportunities to do big things for God. We may preach great sermons, write great books or songs, start churches, give huge amounts of money, pray multiple times a day, be hailed as surely the greatest example of Christianity since Paul the apostle, but if we do not love God with all our hearts, minds, souls and strength, how are we profited and how is He glorified?

If you desire to be a genuine follower of Jesus, you have to follow Him in the self-sacrificing love He had for His Father, so much so that He would die a horrible death at His request.

Can you see that?

Make that the primary goal of your life.

Ask God to make that possible in your life, and to enable you to die to your self sufficiently to accomplish that one life goal.

Once you love Him with that self-abandoning fervency, the Holy Spirit can begin to lead you in doing great things for Him.

Without love as your motive, you will be spinning your wheels, so to speak. But with fervent love for God, you can do all things by the Spirit.

Why? Because faith does not work except by love. (Galatians 5:6)

6. Become a Disciple: Follow Jesus

Jesus was not one to beg people to follow Him.

He actually seemed to dissuade them from doing so, at times.

"The Son of man has no place to lay His head," He told a scribe who declared he would follow Jesus anywhere.

"Let the dead bury their dead: but go thou and preach the kingdom of God," he told another who wanted to wait for his father to die before he left home to follow Jesus.

Jesus was not a salesman, because He was not selling. He was trading. He offered His life in exchange for the petty cares of this world carried by every sinner.

His life? Not an easy, leisurely, stroll in the park, but one that counted every distraction of this world as exactly what it was. Distraction.

Many preachers will not tell you what Jesus told people who professed a desire to follow Him. He said something like, "Oh yeah? Do you really? Well, let me tell you what it's going to cost you."

"Oh, how could it cost to follow Him?" many ask. "Salvation is free!"

Nevertheless, Jesus said to count the cost lest we find that we haven't given sufficient consideration to finishing what we set out to do in following Him. What cost? Giving up everything for Him.

It is no coincidence that immediately after He spoke of counting the cost, He said, "*So likewise, whosoever he be of you that forsaketh not all that he hath, he cannot be my disciple.*"

Many preachers want to sell you a "pig in a poke," as the old folks called a sales pitch that disclosed none of the perceived "hitches" of the purchase.

Jesus was for full disclosure.

Some preachers will tell you how easy it is to say a prayer and get your free pass to heaven.

But Jesus said, "*Strait is the gate, and narrow is the way, which leadeth unto life, and few there be that find it.*" Strait? That means narrow because of obstacles in the path.

The Word of God says other things equally startling to leisure-minded mankind.

"*If any man will come after Me, let him deny himself, and take up his cross daily, and follow Me.*"

"*Except ye eat the flesh of the Son of man, and drink His blood, ye have no life in you.*"

"*He that loveth father or mother more than me is not worthy of me: and he that loveth son or daughter more than me is not worthy of me.*"

If you have ever been to church, I wonder if you have ever been told of the obstacles, the dying to self, the self-denial, the forsaking of "stuff," the hating of this life.

Jesus had no interest in recruiting, in filling seats in a sanctuary. He was not looking for half-hearted, part-time Christians. He wanted people who could see truth, evaluate the real offer, and recognize the fatal end of the path they were on, people who would recognize the Ark of His person as the only rescue from what was to come.

Disciples are not to be hypocrites. They must be all in or all out. Lukewarm is as bad as cold.

And there is no other category of follower but disciple. Disciples were the ones who were so much like Christ that the people of Antioch began to call Jesus' followers "Christians," that is, Christ-like ones.

What about "believers"? Disciples *are* the believers.

What about sons and daughters of God?" Disciples *are* the sons and daughters of God.

What about His followers? Disciples *are* the ones who follow Him.

What about church members? Disciples *are* the Church members.

"Well," you might object, "I love Jesus."

"*If you love Me,*" Jesus said, "*keep My commandments.*"

The apostle John declared this: "*He that saith, 'I know Him,' and keepeth not His commandments, is a liar, and the truth is not in him.*"

No pig in a poke there.

You deserve to know what the landscape of the Kingdom of God looks like. You need to know before you buy the false conclusion that nothing needs to change in your life as a Christian.

Find someone who will tell you straight out the brand of Gospel Jesus preached. Find a congregation of people who heard the truth and gave up whatever was necessary in order to follow Jesus Christ in reality, rather than in a superficial charade of following.

Jesus told His disciples, *"Go and make disciples."*

There is no other brand or category of "believer" except the one who believes with all his or her heart, who believes exactly what Jesus said and did, and who follows Him in thought, word, actions, and lifestyle, as the Holy Spirit enables and leads.

Be His disciple. Then make disciples, as He commanded.

7. Love Your Neighbor the Way You Love Your Self

Just as the first commandment is a mandate, so is this: *"Love your neighbor as you love yourself."*

I want you to see two stories in the Bible that reveal the crucial nature of this mandate.

First, let's look at the story of Lazarus and the rich man, a story many, many people are familiar with. Read the story in Luke 16 if you are unfamiliar with it.

Lazarus, the poor and disabled man, was laid at the gate of the rich man, in the hope the homeowner would have compassion upon him and feed him with *"the crumbs which fell from the rich man's table."*

However, we do not see the rich man

doing anything for the poor wretch at his gate. Only the dogs came, licking his sores.

When both men died, Jesus said the rich man found himself in hell, but the poor man was in the "bosom of Abraham," or Heaven.

The reason?

The only reason given the rich man for his terrible fate was, "*Remember that thou in thy lifetime receivedst thy good things, and likewise Lazarus evil things: but now he is comforted, and thou art tormented.*"

We must conclude that he did not love Lazarus the way he loved himself; he did not do anything to relieve the poor man's burdens.

The second story is that of the sheep and the goats, in Matthew 25. The sheep, being those who provided help and relief to the poor and sick, while the goats did not. Jesus addressed the sheep this way: "*Come, ye blessed of my Father, inherit the kingdom prepared for you from the foundation of the world: for I was an hungred, and ye gave me meat: I was thirsty, and ye gave me drink: I was a stranger, and ye took me in; naked, and ye clothed me: I was sick, and ye visited me: I was in prison, and ye came unto me."*

Jesus considered the care given to these poor, sick, desolate, and homeless as care given directly to Him.

To the goats, who did none of these things, He said, *"Depart from me, ye cursed, into everlasting fire, prepared for the devil and his angels."*

Surely, you see the crucial need for loving your neighbor as you love your self. Please do not miss this vital aspect of your relationship with Jesus Christ.

Many of you have doubtlessly been told that all God expects of you is your belief, and if you took that to mean belief at its most superficial level, you were misinformed.

The belief spoken of in the Bible is the kind that trusts Him so fully that it obeys the two great commandments to love with wild abandonment, forsaking all selfishness.

Even if you could somehow concoct a plan to satisfy the poor and hurting *without* loving God fervently and without loving your neighbor to the degree you love yourself, it would be in vain.

Love is and must be the heart's motive for all that you do. And that kind of love can only be acquired in one's heart by the presence of the Holy Spirit. And the heart is what God judges.

Believe this one thing: there is no way to get around being born again into the Spirit and into loving God and your neighbor through Jesus Christ.

Forsake every tradition and false teaching that suggests otherwise. **Do not be found naked of love when you stand before the King of all kings!**

You can amass fortunes in this life, but you will not have one penny when you stand before God. You can have multitudes of admirers and people who think you are great, but it is only Jesus who must vouch for you on Judgment Day.

What a tragic shame it would be if you worked all your life for temporal peace and prosperity, only to find that it was love for God that you were missing – the only obedience in life that can give you the ability to love your neighbor as you love yourself!

I urge you, friend, to put aside everything that hinders you from loving God with white-hot intensity.

Make the goal of your life to love Him beyond all human belief and ability so that you will be able to love your neighbor as yourself.

8. Be Led by the Holy Spirit

Remember what you read about repentance earlier?

Your human thought patterns are now your enemy. Romans chapter eight says, *"The mind of the flesh is hostile towards God."* (v. 7 WEB)

Your natural mind is an enemy of God!

No matter how intelligent you are – or think you are – you cannot trust your natural mind to lead you. I often hear people say that God gave them a brain in order to think correctly. He certainly did, and then He went one better: He gave Jesus' disciples the mind of Christ, through the presence of the Holy Spirit. And He instructed us to renew our minds, our thinking.

Here are a couple of scripture passages

for explanation:

"Don't be conformed to this world, but be transformed by the renewing of your mind, so that you may prove what is the good, well-pleasing, and perfect will of God." (Romans 12:2 WEB)

You cannot know or do the will of God until you submit your mind to the Word of God and the Holy Spirit for transformation.

"And he that searcheth the hearts knoweth what is the mind of the Spirit, because he maketh intercession for the saints according to the will of God." (*Romans 8:27*)

Therefore, *"Let this mind be in you, which was also in Christ Jesus."* (Philippians 2:5)

The plan of God is for our minds to be renewed to His way of thinking so that we will be led, not by our own understanding, but by the Spirit of God, Who is our Guide. (See John 16:13)

Now, listen to this mandate:

"For as many as are led by the Spirit of God, they are the sons of God. (Romans 8:14)

Read with emphasis on "THEY." The direct inference is that **those who are not led by the Spirit of God are not the children of God**.

Can you see how important it is that we not only have the Spirit of God in us, but that we trust His leading and guidance as He speaks, nudges us and checks us with promptings?

If you continually lean to your own understanding, how can you claim to be a follower of Christ, when the Holy Spirit is the very Spirit of Christ?

We could go on with scriptural foundation for the absolute necessity of following the leading of the Holy Spirit, but if you have doubts, you must pray for wisdom and understanding from Him.

This is a need that must not be set aside or doubted.

Perhaps your peer group would shun you if they knew you claimed to be led by the Spirit of God. That is a very real possibility. But you must ask your self, Who am I here to please, God or men?

Man did not die for you. The high esteem in which some might hold you is valueless if God does not hold you in high esteem with regard to your obedience and love toward Him.

Sever your self from the ties to this earthly culture, and from the opinions of men. Get to know the Holy Spirit of God, and to trust Him explicitly. He will not fail you. If you believe He has failed you, it is you who have not held up your part of the agreement to trust Him and love Him. He has already said, "*I will never leave you nor forsake you.*"

When you receive the fullness of the Holy Spirit, begin to seek His guidance in every circumstance.

Don't hesitate to give your ear to His voice. He will lead you into God's will.

9. Acquire Great Love for Truth

What? Must I love *truth* now, also? Isn't it enough to love God and my neighbor fervently?

You might say loving truth comes with the territory, and one of the symptoms of not loving the truth is not having a great desire to read and live by the written Word of God.

First, let's clarify what truth we are talking about.

Worldly truth is often related to facts, which might be temporal. For example, it may be true that, today, you are a home builder, and the facts most relevant to you are city and county building codes. If in the future, building codes change, then, for you, some of the facts have changed.

The truth we are talking about is

foundational truth: there is truly a God; He is the God of Abraham, Isaac, Jacob and of Jesus Christ; His will and the history of His involvement with mankind have been recorded in the Old Testament and the New, and they contain wisdom for living in this world, and specifically, how man may arrive at eternally blissful life rather than harsh judgment.

This represents truth from God's perspective, not from man's.

If you truly love God, you will trust and love His written Word, which is truth. I feel confident in saying that if you have a problem loving and trusting His truth (His Word), you will have a problem loving and trusting God Himself. (The evidence of that will be your level of obedience to His commandments.)

If someone tells you that you can be led by the Holy Spirit **apart from** reading the Word, do not listen to that person. He is a maverick with resistance to the scriptures and/or whose reliance is on his or her own understanding.

Jesus said *He* is *"the Way, the Truth and the Life and that no man comes unto the Father"* except through Him.

Loving Jesus should automatically give you a love for God's written Word, for, as you might know, Jesus IS the Word of God. (See John 1.)

Just as loving God is quantifiable, from God's perspective, and He desires all our love, so is love for truth quantifiable, and it must have no limits. Limited love for both God and truth will cease when the limit has been reached, resulting in a cessation of pursuing the same.

God's love and His truth cannot be plumbed for a finite depth. Men who approach God with a finite love for Him and His truth will surely find an end to both.

"Ah but," some say, "Why do you need the written Word when you have the Living Word of Christ in the Holy Spirit?"

Too many false teachers and deceitful workers are out there, and it is written that *"Satan himself is transformed into an angel of light.*" It is too easy to be influenced by the subtle lies of the enemy, especially if you have not yet gained a level of spiritual maturity sufficient to discern lying spirits.

The written Word of God has been inspired by the Holy Spirit, and it serves as "guardrails" to confirm what we hear from the Holy Spirit and deny what we hear from deceitful humans.

2 Timothy 3:16 declares, "***All scripture*** *is given by inspiration of God, and is profitable for doctrine, for reproof, for correction, for instruction in righteousness.*"

Jesus was fond of quoting scripture by announcing, "*It is written...*" And He told Pharisees who were trying to twist scripture, "*Ye do err, not knowing the scriptures, nor the power of God.*"

There are those who discount New Testament writings as scripture, but Peter says this of Paul's letters, "*As also in all his epistles, speaking in them of these things; in which are some things hard to be understood, which they that*

are unlearned and unstable wrest
[pervert]*, as they do also **the other
scriptures**, unto their own destruction.*"
(2 Peter 3:16)

Now that we have established the
validity of scriptural truth, do we know
whether loving truth is a mandate?

Paul said of those who followed false
teachers and false prophets, "*They
received not the love of the truth, that
they might be saved.*" (2 Thessalonians)

The phrase, "*...that they might be
saved,*" tells us that love for truth is not
optional. How can one who does not love
truth believe the Gospel enough to give
his or her life to the control of the Holy
Spirit?

And note that the apostle says, they did
not *receive* love for truth. If you are
deficient in your love for truth, know
that you may receive greater love for
truth by asking God for it.

Some people really do not care about
truth. Others are ambivalent, meaning
that they might prefer truth to outright

lies, but when truth becomes inconvenient, they would prefer not to have to deal with it.

The trouble with people who do not love truth is that they will stop insisting on truth at whatever level their love or preference for it runs out. And beyond that, they are ripe for deception.

But those who love truth fervently will absolutely not settle for a half-truth or any kind of deception.

If you don't currently regard truth so highly that you love it, you would be wise to begin asking the Lord to give you a great love for it.

Otherwise, deception is waiting for you.

10. Make Disciples

"Go ye therefore, and teach all nations, baptizing them in the name of the Father, and of the Son, and of the Holy Ghost: **teaching them to observe all things whatsoever I have commanded you."**
Matthew 28:19-20

In chapter six, we tried to make it clear that there are no part-time followers of Jesus Christ, despite the many sweet sermons to the contrary.

When Jesus told His original disciples to go and make more disciples, He did not describe any other kind of follower. In fact, after Jesus commanded those men to make disciples, He added this: *"teaching them to observe all things whatsoever I have commanded you."*

All disciples are to observe all things Jesus commanded His original disciples, including to go and make disciples.

What am I saying?

That if you are a disciple of Jesus, you need to make other disciples.

What? Do I have to make disciples? How am I supposed to know how to do that?

If you ARE a disciple, you surely must recall how you got to be one. If you don't recall becoming a disciple, do not try to make disciples until you know that you are one.

The process, as Jesus demonstrated it, is to teach in the midst of personal relationship. It is not sterile, classroom teaching. (I.E., if it involves classroom teaching, it must not be sterile, or devoid of personal relationship.) The discipleship process should show new believers how to rid themselves of the weighty baggage of temporal life, how to overcome the flesh, introduce them to personal relationship with God through the presence of the Holy Spirit, and teach them how to engage with the plans of the Spirit of God. It must focus on reaching the lost with the love of God and His Word.

If you are not yet a mature disciple of Jesus, begin to focus your efforts on finding out what that means and how to employ God's gifts to you for His glory.

Your love for your neighbors as yourself will urge you to desire the best for others. Love is motive enough – or ought to be – to make the effort to begin the process of making disciples.

11. Forgive Everybody, Everything

People who have difficulty forgiving others believe they have a right to withhold forgiveness.

Let me make this very harsh statement concerning such a right: everyone has the right to spend eternity in torment. Those who are wise will forgo that right.

How is eternal torment related to unforgiveness?

Jesus offered forgiveness of sin to all the world, with the object of acceptance being eternal life from the sentence of condemnation pronounced upon all mankind. However, many, inexplicably, believe that it is more important to hold onto what they have of worldliness, though its end is eternal destruction.

One of the stipulations for receiving that forgiveness is that, upon accepting the offer, the recipients must then forgive others just as readily as they received forgiveness.

Jesus describes a situation in Matthew 18 whereby a master forgives one of his servants a huge debt, and that servant turns around and has someone jailed for his inability to repay him a very small debt.

In that account, the original servant's debt was ten thousand talents of gold or silver, whereas, the debt he would not forgive was "one hundred pence."

We need to apply some scale to the two debts. A talent was a weight of gold or silver equivalent to about 48 pounds, according to some experts, and the servant's debt was for ten thousand of them. The amount owed to that servant, however, was equivalent to fourteen dollars.

The first debt was an inestimably large amount, as though it could be compared to the inestimable value of our forgiveness of sin.

Suffice it to say that, because of the huge forgiveness we have received, we owe forgiveness to everyone else; no forgiveness required of us toward others could come close to equaling the debt we have been forgiven by Christ.

Jesus said this: *"If you do not forgive, neither will your Father which is in heaven forgive your trespasses."*

You cannot value eternal life very highly if you refuse to forgive.

What? Do you think it is unfair of God to withhold forgiveness from you if you refuse it to others? Why? Because He is God, and far better able to forgive than you are?

That will not fly as an excuse to retain unforgiveness. God offers you grace to forgive, unless you refuse to humble yourself and ask Him for it. Jesus said that *"with God, all things are possible."*

I take this opportunity to urge you: do not withhold forgiveness from anyone, no matter how heinous you consider his or her crime against you.

Jesus said, this: *"Freely you have received; freely give."*

There is no justice to be had in unforgiveness. The one you refuse to forgive will not be long harmed, or hindered from Heaven by your stubbornness.

Forgive freely, and free your own soul from the roadblock to Heaven that unforgiveness produces.

Forgiveness is a mandate of God's Kingdom.

12. Do God's Will, Not Your Own

Your own will was once of utmost concern to you. Say, when you were between two and four years old, especially.

It was probably in that time that you learned the personal satisfaction of having your own way in life.

Perhaps that desire for personal satisfaction served you well for years afterward, maybe even all your life. It could be that people learned you were so self-centered and self-indulgent that it was not pleasant to disagree with you or cross you.

Have you been so unfortunate in life that you always got your way? People whose self-will is of supreme importance to them do exist. But generally, they are the only ones in their circle of associates who are happy about it.

The thing most needful for all of us is to place this life in a set of scales to be balanced against the value of eternity. You know, 80 to100 years of this life versus unlimited life afterward; temporal happiness versus eternal bliss; cheap counterfeits of temporal value versus the true riches eternally.

We established in chapter five that He created you out of clay and that He *is* God; you're not. While you have your set of scales out, place your will on one side and God's on the other. How does that look to you?

Hopefully, you are fully in agreement that your will matters little in the grand scheme of His will.

It is safe to say that people who always go about doing their own will will never accomplish God's will.

We should have more respect for our Creator than to ignore His will so that we might be temporarily thought of as important, at least in our own minds.

Some might object, How can I even know

God's will?

If you have a Bible, you can know His general will for your life. Just look at the commandments of Jesus, if you want to know. There are two: Love Him with all your heart, all your mind, all your soul and all your strength. And love your neighbor as you love your self.

Are those impossible? Yes, if you try to do them in your own ability. But just as forgiveness becomes possible by God's grace, so does obedience to His commandments.

Again, there are no excuses.

Jesus said that *"Not everyone who says to Me, 'Lord, Lord,' shall enter the Kingdom of Heaven, but he who does the will of My Father in Heaven."*

Calling Jesus "Lord" is not uncommon among men. Treating Him as Lord, unfortunately, *is* uncommon. The word, "Lord," presumes supreme authority to the one so-called. That means, His authority to direct your life is greater than your authority to direct your own life. In order for that to be reality, you and I have to humble our selves. Completely.

That is offensive to a person who loves his or her own life.

If you truly understand that doing His will is a mandate of God, you will humble your self completely to Him, and you will call on Him to enable you to do the impossible commandments of Jesus.

That is, you will love Him with all of your being, and thus, be enabled to love your neighbor as your self.

Until you love Him that much, you cannot give up your own will in order to do His.

Is Heaven worth denying your self the pleasure of doing your own will for a few decades, until temporal life is over?

You bet your life it is!

13. Ask God to Chastise You

I heard that laugh!

It echoed all the way from my own childhood, when I avoided chastisement with every fiber of my being.

What child would ever have the intuitive heart of a mature follower of Christ, so much so that he or she would say to his natural father or mother, "Please give me a spanking; I need it"?

But surely a mature follower of Jesus Christ would invite his Father to chastise him!

Right?

No? Do you mean you have not asked God to chastise you?

Well, does He chastise you anyway? If so, that's a great thing. No, it is not pleasant when He chastises. But it produces *"the peaceable fruit of righteousness unto them which are exercised thereby."*

One of the most dangerous situations in this life is one in which God is not chastising you. Of that situation, the writer of Hebrews says, *"If ye are without chastening, whereof all have been made partakers, then are ye bastards, and not sons."* (12:8 ASV)

I'm not sure it could be stated any plainer than that.

If you find your self in that situation, ASK God to chastise you. It might not seem pleasant but it is instruction, and, in fact, it is course correction.

If you were driving across the country and someone told you that you were on the wrong road, it might not be pleasant to turn around and backtrack, but wouldn't it be better than arriving at the wrong destination?

Chastisement does that; it is done to prevent you from arriving at the wrong destination.

Don't think it is odd that chastisement should be mandated by the Lord.

No one is perfect, needing no course correction. We all need it.

Yet, if you take exception to that concept and resist chastisement, you disqualify your self as a son or daughter of God.

Wouldn't you much *"rather be in subjection unto the Father of spirits, and live?"* (v. 9)

You can "kick against the pricks" all you like, but after all is said and done, you must receive correction from the Lord if you expect to have eternal life with Him.

14. Be Rich Toward God

Who in this country has not wanted to be rich at one time or another?

Being rich makes one wise and popular, doesn't it? And isn't that what life is all about?

Actually, no.

While many Christians tout the glories of wealth, the Bible cautions us about it.

First of all, Jesus said riches are deceitful. Not that riches have awareness, to actively deceive, but the desire for and possession of riches tend to deceive the ones desiring them.

How can riches deceive?

The most prominent deceit of wealth is in comforting its possessors, conditioning them to think that riches are security. People seem to need reminding that God is our security, He alone and entirely.

Go ahead and ask me: Wouldn't you rather have money than be broke? Yes.

But the Christian's stance ought to be wholly based on God's written Word. It cautions us, *"Don't weary yourself to be rich. In your wisdom, show restraint. Why do you set your eyes on that which is not? For it certainly sprouts wings like an eagle and flies in the sky."* (Proverbs 23:4-5 WEB)

As for those who justify seeking wealth because they say Jesus was wealthy, I say, be careful that you do not deceive yourself. Show me where Jesus sought wealth. He is the One who said He had no place to lay His head, the One who, when He desired to pay the temple tax, received a donation from a fish, and who, when He made His triumphant entry into Jerusalem, borrowed a donkey.

Jesus' idea of real wealth, according to Luke 16, was possessing what He called "the true riches," which have little to do with worldly riches, or "unrighteous mammon."

God's counsel to us is that *"godliness with contentment is great gain,"* and so, we should withdraw ourselves from people for whom *"godliness is a means of gain."* (1 Timothy 6)

If money is not "true riches," what is?

True riches are those things and conditions that increase us in the character of Jesus Christ, all that God freely offers us of His vast wealth. Does God use money in Heaven? It's useless there. It's useful here on earth, for our survival needs and those of our neighbors, but when our desire is to consume riches *"upon our lusts,"* riches cease to be among things God desires to bless us with (James 4:3). Money, according to Luke's Gospel, is *"that which is least."*

When we desire the wealth of earth over the wealth of Heaven, we show our priorities to be earth-bound.

Colossians 3:1-2 tells us, *"If then you were raised together with Christ, seek the things that are above, where Christ is, seated on the right hand of God. Set your mind on the things that are above, not on the things that are on the earth."*

And Jesus affirms that, saying, *"How difficult it is for those who have riches to enter into the Kingdom of God!"* (Mark 10:23 WEB)

In His hallmark address advocating trust in God, Jesus said, *"Lay not up for yourselves treasures upon earth, where moth and rust doth corrupt, and where thieves break through and steal: But lay up for yourselves treasures in heaven, where neither moth nor rust doth corrupt, and where thieves do not break through nor steal."* (Matthew 6:19-20)

At the end of that chapter, He summed up His point: *"Seek ye first the kingdom of God, and his righteousness; and all these things shall be added unto you."*

That point is worth reiterating: Don't labor to be rich. If you labor to meet your family's needs and to help others, that is pleasing to God. But make your priority to *"Seek first the Kingdom of God and His righteousness."* Do that, and trust that your Father will supply everything you need.

Do you recall the story Jesus told about the rich farmer? When his harvest prospered and he had a large surplus, he thought only of himself and his comfort.

He said, *"I will pull down my barns, and build greater; and there will I bestow all my fruits and my goods. And I will say to my soul, 'Soul, thou hast much goods laid up for many years; take thine ease, eat, drink, and be merry.'"*

God did not say to him, "Well done! You've increased what I gave you."

Instead, He said, *"Thou fool, this night thy soul shall be required of thee: then whose shall those things be, which thou hast provided?"*

Jesus added this: *"So is he that layeth up treasure for himself, and is not rich toward God."*

You may certainly disagree with what I am about to say, but this is what I hear from Scripture: Every good gift He places in our trust is given because we are to be stewards of His manifold grace. Every gift is not just for our pleasure, but also for others, in that we are to love our neighbors as ourselves.

Being "rich toward God" is not just dropping a twenty into the offering at church; it is as Jesus said, "*Inasmuch as ye have done it unto one of the least of these My brethren, ye have done it unto Me.*"

Now, because so many people professing Christianity are still trusting money for their security, I'm going to add a list of additional scriptures to support what has already been said here:

- "*Riches profit not in the day of wrath: but righteousness delivereth from death.*" (Proverbs 11:4)

- "*He that trusteth in his riches shall fall: but the righteous shall flourish as a branch.*" (Proverbs 11:28)

- *"And the cares of this world, and the deceitfulness of riches, and the lusts of other things entering in, choke the word, and it becometh unfruitful."* (Mark 4:19)

- *"And he said unto them, Take heed, and beware of covetousness: for a man's life consisteth not in the abundance of the things which he possesseth."* (Luke 12:15)

- *"And having food and raiment let us be therewith content."* (1 Timothy 6:8)

- *"But they that will be rich fall into temptation and a snare, and into many foolish and hurtful lusts, which drown men in destruction and perdition."* (1 Timothy 6:9)

- *"For the love of money is the root of all evil: which while some coveted after, they have erred from the faith, and pierced themselves through with many sorrows."* (1 Timothy 6:10)

- *"Charge them that are rich in this world, that they be not highminded, nor trust in uncertain riches, but in the living God, who giveth us richly all things to enjoy; that they do good, that they be rich in good works, ready to distribute, willing to communicate; laying up in store for themselves a good foundation against the time to come, that they may lay hold on eternal life."* (1 Timothy 6:17-19)

- *"But whoso hath this world's good, and seeth his brother have need, and shutteth up his bowels of compassion from him, how dwelleth the love of God in him?"* (1 John 3:17)

The final word is this, *"if riches increase, set not your heart upon them."* Let riches come to us as God desires, not as our flesh will desire. And then, ask Him what He wants done with them.

Don't be a fool for riches. Be rich toward God by using them as He directs.

15. Live in the Secret Place

Men have always longed for a place of peace and quiet, their own little paradise, like a piece of Heaven here on earth. Buddhists have called it "Shangri La;" others have called it "Nirvana," or "Utopia."

To satisfy this yearning, men have worked hard and long to have second homes in the mountains or by a body of water. They have invented "man caves," fishing clubs, retirement villages, and more, all for a small slice of heavenly peace.

The first such place that ever existed – and really, the model for that genre – was not man's idea, but God's. He called it Eden. It was a garden set apart to be actual Heaven on earth, with the loving Creator as the Host who provided every need, including the love, joy, and peace that everyone craves, and the sweetness of His fellowship with never a worry or fear.

Well, sin blew that!

But God was not finished with the idea.

He set aside a place He called the Secret Place. It answers the need in everyone's heart, fills the void destroyed by sin, and restores personal fellowship with the God who desires to be Father, Provider, Protector, and King to those who love Him.

The Psalmist, speaking by the Spirit of God, described the Secret Place as a sanctuary, much like a wildlife sanctuary where no hunter or trapper is allowed, but for humankind, instead, with peace and protection from every enemy, for all men, women, and children who would entrust themselves to the Lord God Almighty, Maker of Heaven and earth.

Perhaps this Secret Place was the thought behind the man-made sanctuaries some call houses of God, with steeples, stages, pulpits, and padded seating. But the true Secret Place is not man-made, nor is it man-run and operated. And it is a very real sanctuary, a place safe from every conceivable attack by the enemy of your soul.

Where is it?

It is in the intimate presence of God. Accessible by His genuine family members, those bought and paid for by the blood of Jesus Christ, those who, by their knowledge of that fact, submit to His Lordship in the most genuine of terms.

Of this place, Jesus said, *"When you pray, enter into your inner chamber, and having shut your door, pray to your Father who is in secret, and your Father who sees in secret will reward you openly."* Only, the "inner chamber" and the "door" may be literal or figurative, so that no matter where you are, you can leave behind all the cares of this world, and come into His very real presence.

We believe it was David who penned the

Secret Place message from the Father, in Psalm 91, having known of it in the days when he played his harp unto God in the peaceful shepherd fields of Israel.

It is sad to realize that so many people are seeking in the world what God offers freely in His presence: love, joy, peace, patience, gentleness, goodness, faithfulness, meekness, and self-control. But they look in all the wrong places and pay dearly for counterfeits.

The invitation into this sanctuary is open: *"Come boldly unto the throne of grace, that we may obtain mercy, and find grace to help in time of need."*

Just wear your best: a robe of righteousness, cleansed with the blood of Jesus Christ that He shed for you.

In the Secret Place, you have nothing to fear. No disease, no pestilence, no fiery darts of the enemy. Just pure peace and love in His presence. And best of all, you never have to leave; you may live there full time.

Read Psalm 91. And make your home

the Secret Place of His presence.

16. Pursue Holiness, the Character of Christ

"Holiness" is a taboo word in many Christian circles because when it is used in a sentence that implies that a recipient of Christ's salvation must be holy, they immediately get their hackles up.

Almost every Christian knows that, without holiness, "*no man shall see the Lord.*" The rub is, *whose* holiness: the saved or the Savior's? That is a concern at all because so many Christians have become convinced they do not have to participate in the holiness of God.

At this point, it would be good to lay down your weapons of traditional thinking and man-made doctrines, for here, we will be examining the Word of God.

The first need is to settle the question raised above: whose holiness does God want us to bring into His presence? The answer I find in scripture is: Both, Jesus and we, with sanctified hearts. As it is written, *"Who shall ascend into the hill of the LORD? Or who shall stand in his holy place? He that hath clean hands, and a pure heart; who hath not lifted up his soul unto vanity, nor sworn deceitfully."* (Psalm 24: 3-4)

Some American pastors and evangelists have become fond of inviting people into the Kingdom of God with an offer something like this: "Just say this prayer and you will have eternal life." (And at times, without even a prayer: "Just raise your hand...")

Please be aware that this practice is never seen or hinted at in scripture.

The reason I bring this up is that the kind of altar call described above represents a sort of minimalist thinking that treats salvation as if God expects absolutely nothing of you as a follower of Christ. If you have read the previous fifteen chapters of this book, you should know that assumption is not true.

Commitment to Jesus Christ is an offer to give up your old life in exchange for taking on the life of Christ.

Isaiah 61:10 says, *"I will greatly rejoice in the LORD, my soul shall be joyful in my God; for he hath clothed me with the garments of salvation, he hath covered me with the robe of righteousness, as a bridegroom decketh himself with ornaments, and as a bride adorneth herself with her jewels."*

This tells us that Christ accords to us His robe of righteousness. When He does that, He is affirming that His blood was applied to our sins, making us righteous in the eyes of God.

Without this accorded righteousness, He could not give us the Holy Spirit, whose work in us is to produce holiness IN us, and not just accorded to us.

Ask yourself this question: How is it possible that the Holy Spirit of God could live inside a human for the duration of the person's life <u>without producing some degree of holiness in that person</u>?

Yet, that is what many people believe. They assume that the Holy Spirit will be given to indwell them, but without having any effect on the inward or outward life of the person being indwelled.

Turn that idea around and imagine what would happen in the life of any human if he or she was indwelled by satan or his demons. Certainly, we are all familiar with the effects of demonic oppression and possession.

Why would we think the dead-raising power of the Spirit of God would have no effect toward holiness when He possesses us?

That's an absurd idea.

Zechariah, the father of John Baptist, when he was filled with the Holy Spirit, prophesied, that those who had been redeemed in salvation would serve Christ *"In holiness and righteousness before him, all the days of our life."*

In the Beatitudes, Jesus told His disciples, *"Be ye therefore perfect, even as your Father which is in heaven is perfect."*

Peter, in his first epistle to the Church, admonished followers of Jesus, *"As He which hath called you is holy, so be ye holy in all manner of conversation; because it is written, Be ye holy; for I am holy."*

Paul, in his second letter to the Corinthians, told them, *"Having therefore these promises, dearly beloved, let us cleanse ourselves from all filthiness of the flesh and spirit, perfecting holiness in the fear of God."*

Holiness that we gain from the presence of the Holy Spirit is something we submit to and cooperate with Him in, to the extent that, by His power and by the grace of God, we *cleanse ourselves* from fleshly life.

Understand that Peter was speaking to people who had already committed themselves to Christ, who had been accorded Christ's "robe of righteousness," yet and still, telling them to be holy.

We should know that the process of saved people becoming holy in their lives is called sanctification. (The verb, "sanctify," means to make holy.)

With that in mind, hear what Paul says to the Thessalonians: "*This is the will of God, even your sanctification, that ye should abstain from fornication: that every one of you should know how to possess his vessel in sanctification and honor; ...For God hath not called us unto uncleanness, but unto holiness.*" (1 Thessalonians 4:3-4, 7)

Many have been misinformed by man-made doctrine that teaches you don't have to do anything after being saved, that God's only expectation of you is that you have prayed "the prayer of salvation," even though there is no prayer of salvation in the Bible.

The summary goes all the way back to Hebrews 12:14: "*Follow peace with all men, and holiness, without which no man shall see the Lord.*"

Traditional beliefs don't often require a lot of thinking for someone to hold them. They are often accepted on face value, as told by a beloved relative or respected leader, without the urging of the recipient to search scripture for verification. And because the person believes the doctrines based on high regard for a person rather than high regard for Biblical truth, and they don't want to oppose or offend the person, traditional thinking can be difficult to remove and replace with truth.

Yet the statement of the passage above makes personal holiness a mandate.

Give up the traditional concept that all you have to do is believe (even in the most minimal way) and say a prayer in order to go to Heaven. We have already seen that, in order to be saved, you must be born again, do the will of God, be chastised for course correction, be led by the Holy Spirit, and have a love for the truth! (Re-visit Chapter 9 for more scriptural support of that last mandate.)

Love for truth will produce in you a tireless pursuit of truth through scripture. And it will instill in you a desire to be changed into the kind of holy person God wants you to be.

Let go of anything that opposes personal holiness through the presence of the Holy Spirit of God.

And may God's Holy Spirit lead and guide you to live His life rather than your own, from this day and forever.

# # # #

ABOUT THE AUTHOR

Patrick McWhorter lives in Flowery Branch, Georgia, with his wife, Laurie. The couple's adult sons and daughters-in-law live nearby. They also have a beautiful granddaughter.

Additional copies of this book, as well as his others, may be **ordered online at www.amazon.com**. If your local bookstore does not stock them, request they order the book(s) you desire.

Most of these are also available as eBooks through Amazon.

NON-FICTION
Faith is a Three-Legged Stool
Twenty-One Holes in Once Saved, Always
    Saved
40 Questions to Ask Yourself Before
    Judgment Day
The Planting of the Lord: Discipleship 101
8 Things God Expects of You

The Little Book of Crucial Understanding
FATWALL, Pursuing the Character of Christ

FICTION
Holy Joe
At First Sight
Reward of the Wicked
Where the Rivers Flow

Made in the USA
Columbia, SC
16 June 2020

10501626R00057